Solos, Duets, and Trios

Favorite Cole Porter Classics

Arranged by Tony Esposito

A L T O   S A X

Project Manager: Tony Esposito

FOREWORD

The fifteen pieces in FAVORITE COLE PORTER CLASSICS can successfully be played as Solos or Duets or Trios, WITH OR WITHOUT piano accompaniment. Any combination of these instruments—Flute, Clarinet, Trombone, Trumpet, and Alto Sax—may be used, although some mixes will be better than others.

Also, the following instruments can participate:

BOOK
FLUTE
CLARINET
ALTO SAXOPHONE
TRUMPET
TROMBONE
PIANO ACCOMPANIMENT

FIRST LINE

SECOND LINE

THIRD LINE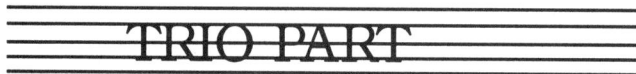

Rehearsal numbers are indicated in all parts to save rehearsal time.

Solos, Duets, and Trios

Favorite Cole Porter Classics

Arranged by Tony Esposito

A L T O   S A X

CONTENTS

ANYTHING GOES

Eb ALTO SAXOPHONE

Words and Music by
COLE PORTER
Arranged by TONY ESPOSITO

Moderately fast

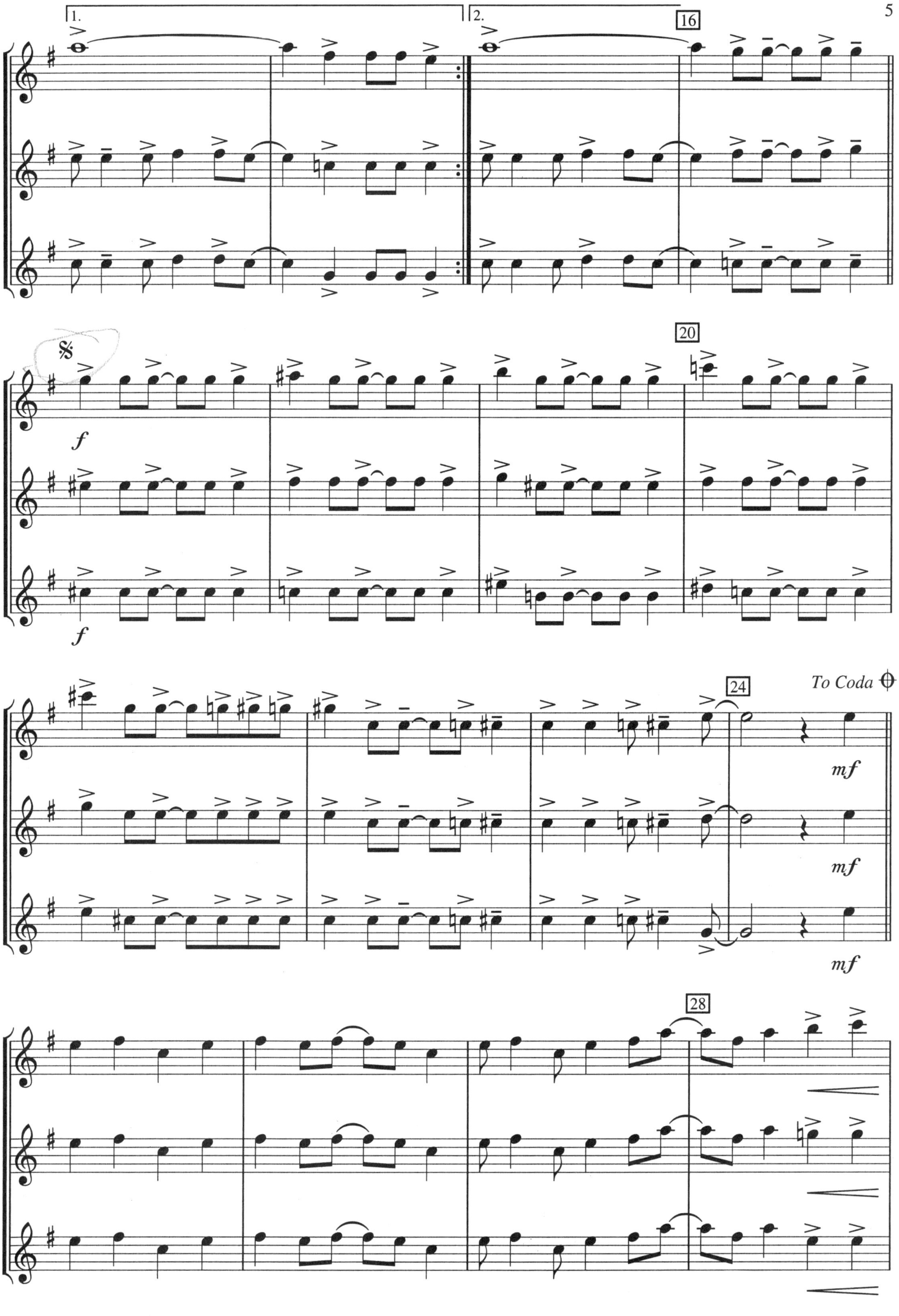
1.
2.
16
20
24
28
To Coda
f
mf

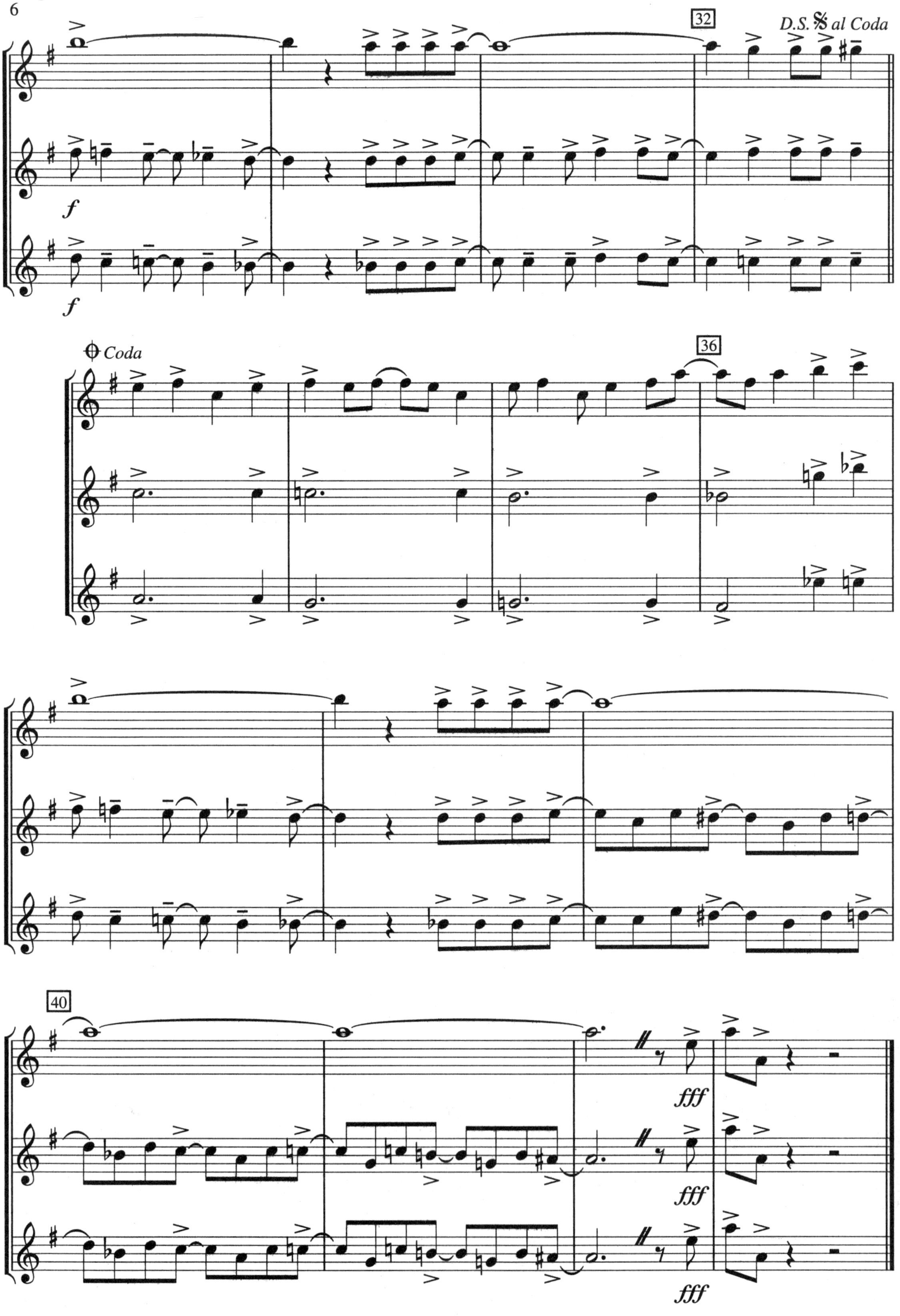
32
D.S. 𝄋 al Coda
f
f
Coda
36
40
fff
fff
fff

AT LONG LAST LOVE

E♭ ALTO SAXOPHONE

Words and Music by
COLE PORTER
Arranged by TONY ESPOSITO

8

Pno. solo
40
2
opt. play
ff
44
Pno. solo
48
mf
52
D.S. 𝄋 al Coda
𝄌 Coda
opt.
56

BEGIN THE BEGUINE

Eb ALTO SAXOPHONE
French Version by
EMELIA RENAUD
Spanish Version by
MARIA GREVER

Words and Music by
COLE PORTER
Arranged by TONY ESPOSITO

Moderate beguine

Begin the Beguine - 5 - 1
IF9810

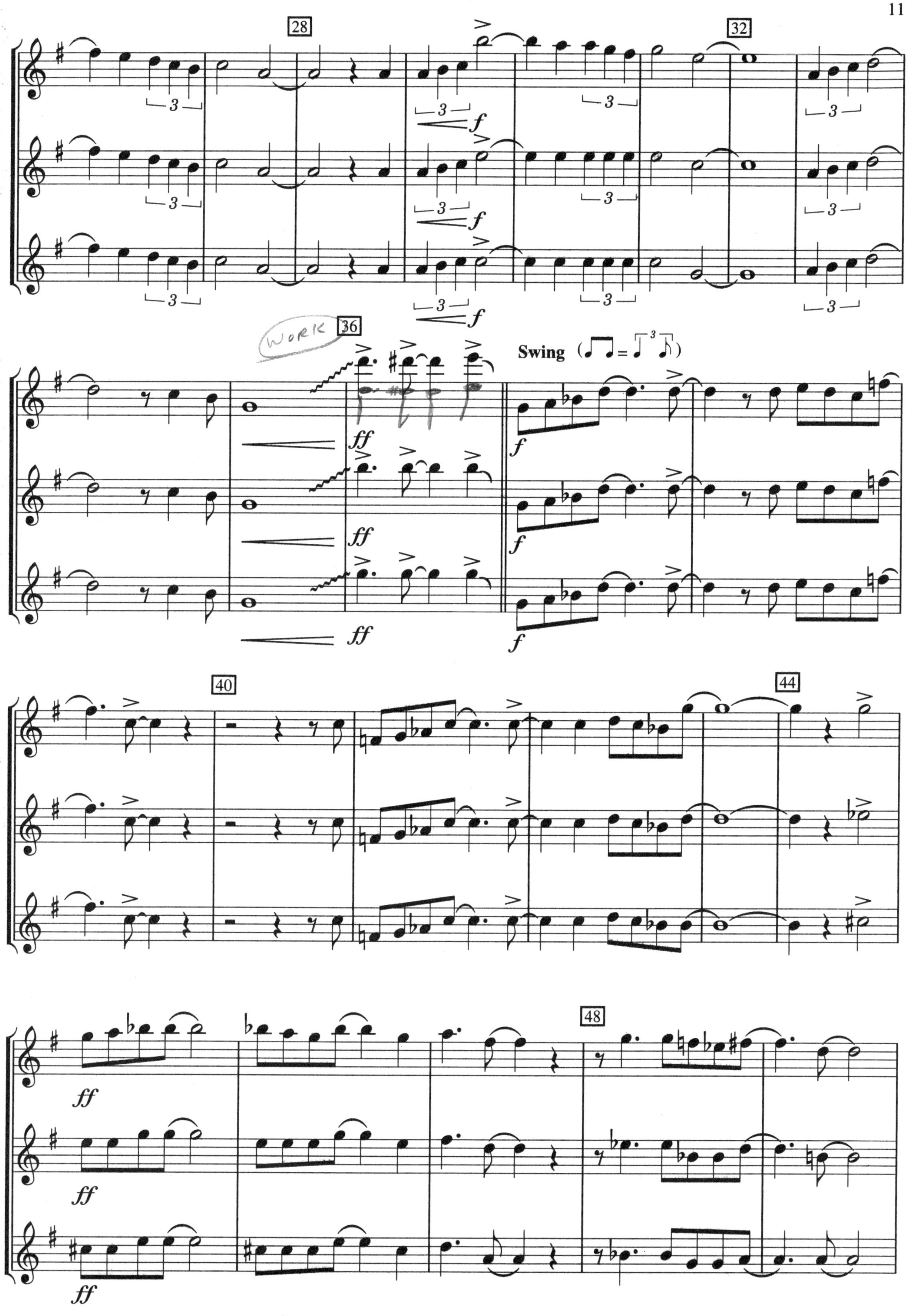
28
32
WORK
36
Swing
40
44
48

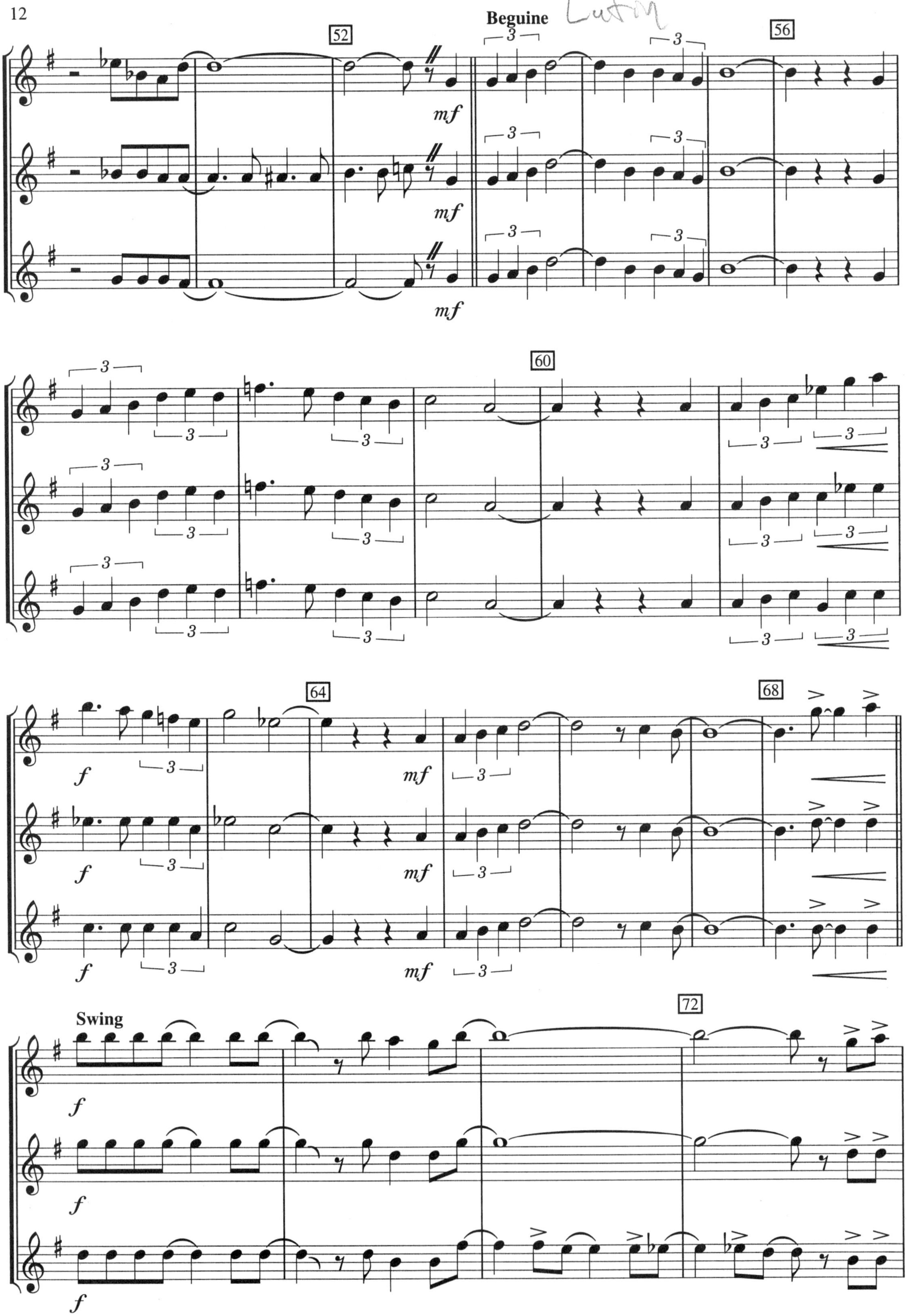
Beguine
52
56
mf
60
64
68
f
mf
Swing
72
f

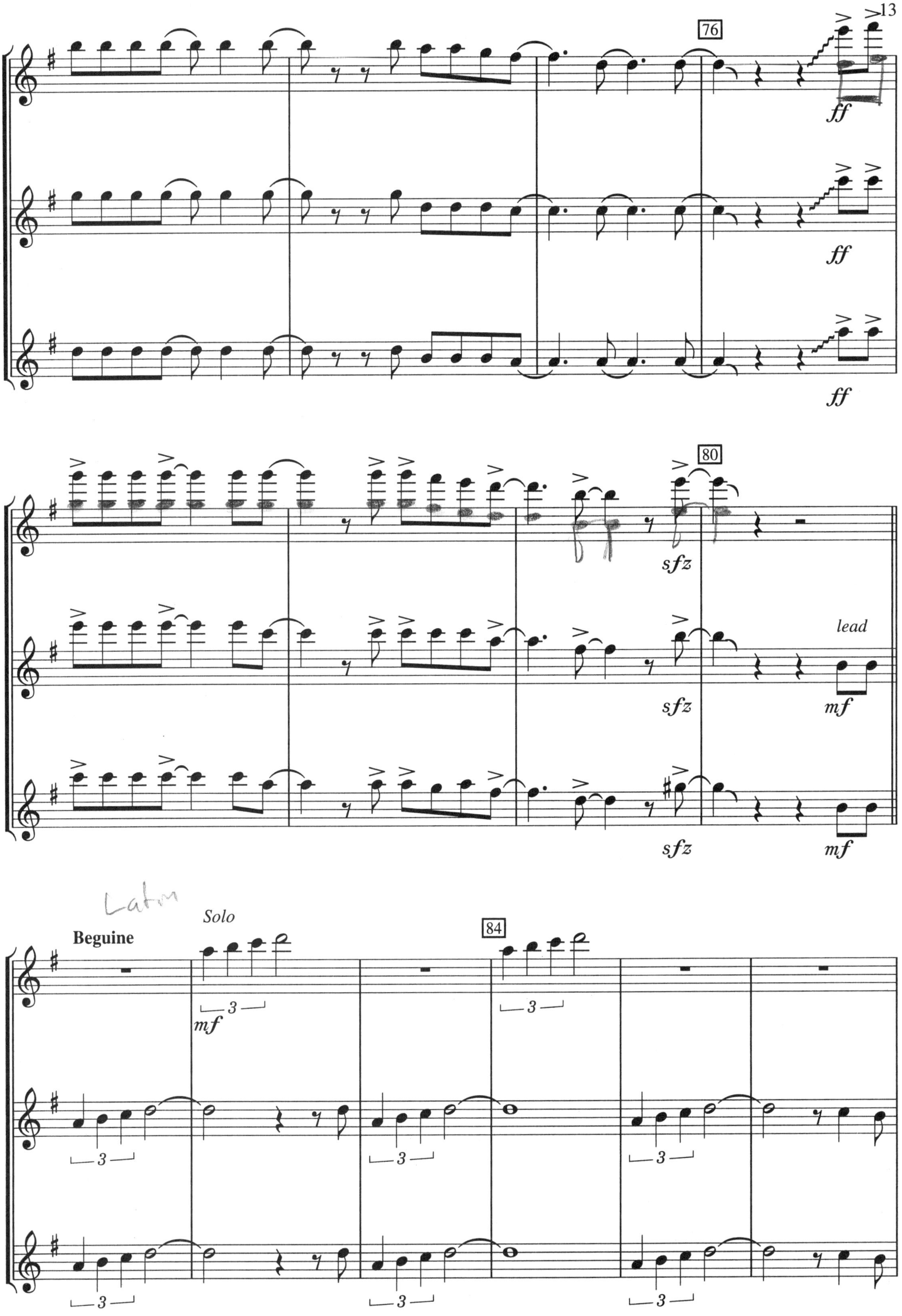
76
ff
ff
ff
80
sfz
sfz
lead
mf
sfz
mf
Beguine
Solo
84
mf
3

14

I GET A KICK OUT OF YOU

Eb ALTO SAXOPHONE

Words and Music by
COLE PORTER
Arranged by TONY ESPOSITO

I Get a Kick Out of You - 3 - 1
IF9810

I Get a Kick Out of You - 3 - 2
IF9810

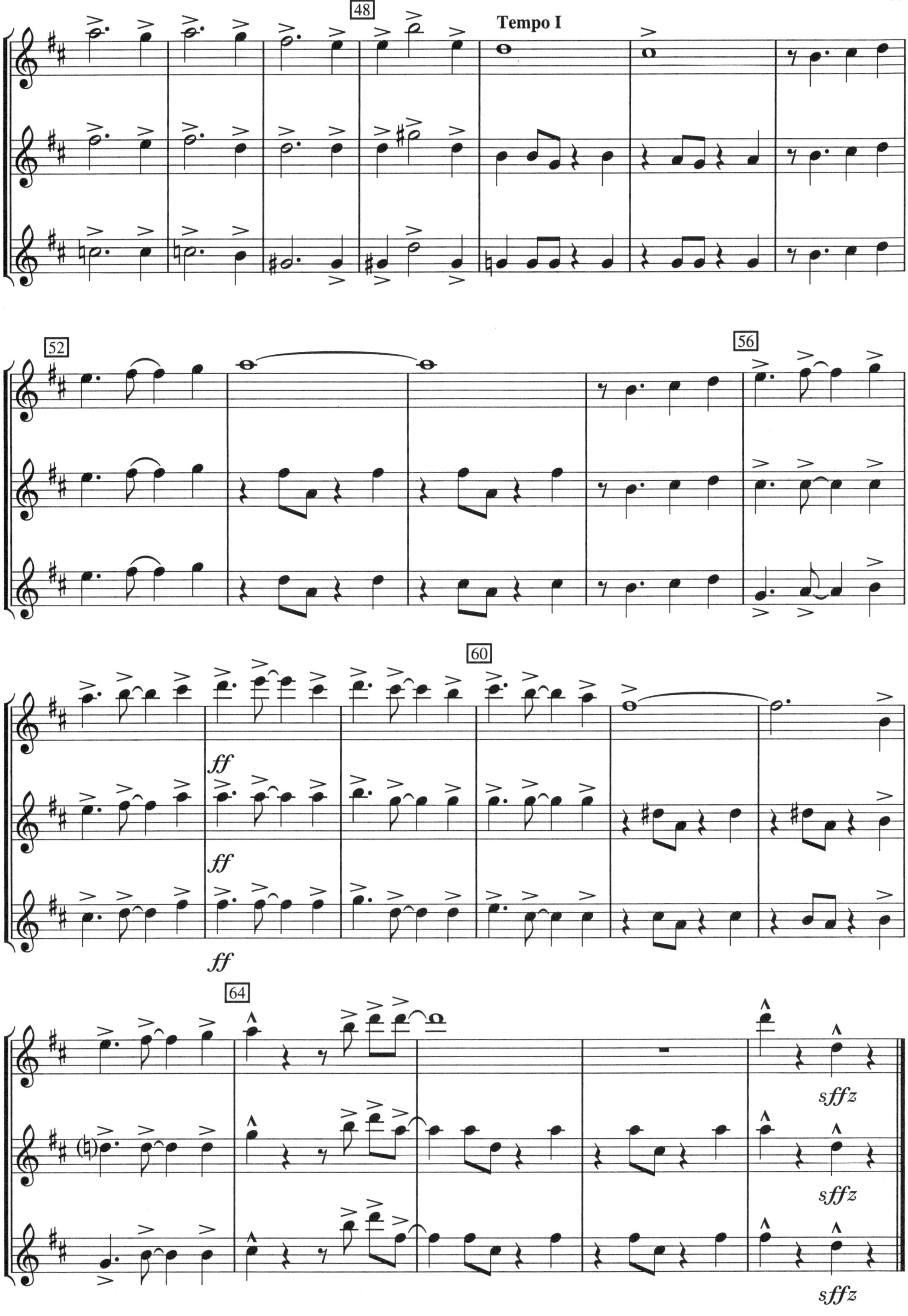
48
Tempo I
52
56
60
ff
ff
ff
64
sffz
sffz
sffz

IT'S ALRIGHT WITH ME

Eb ALTO SAXOPHONE

Words and Music by
COLE PORTER
Arranged by TONY ESPOSITO

It's Alright With Me - 2 - 1
IF9810

It's Alright With Me - 2 - 2
IF9810

Eb ALTO SAXOPHONE

IT'S DE-LOVELY

Words and Music by
COLE PORTER
Arranged by TONY ESPOSITO

It's De-Lovely - 2 - 2
IF9810

JUST ONE OF THOSE THINGS

Eb ALTO SAXOPHONE

Words and Music by
COLE PORTER
Arranged by TONY ESPOSITO

Just One of Those Things - 2 - 1
IF9810

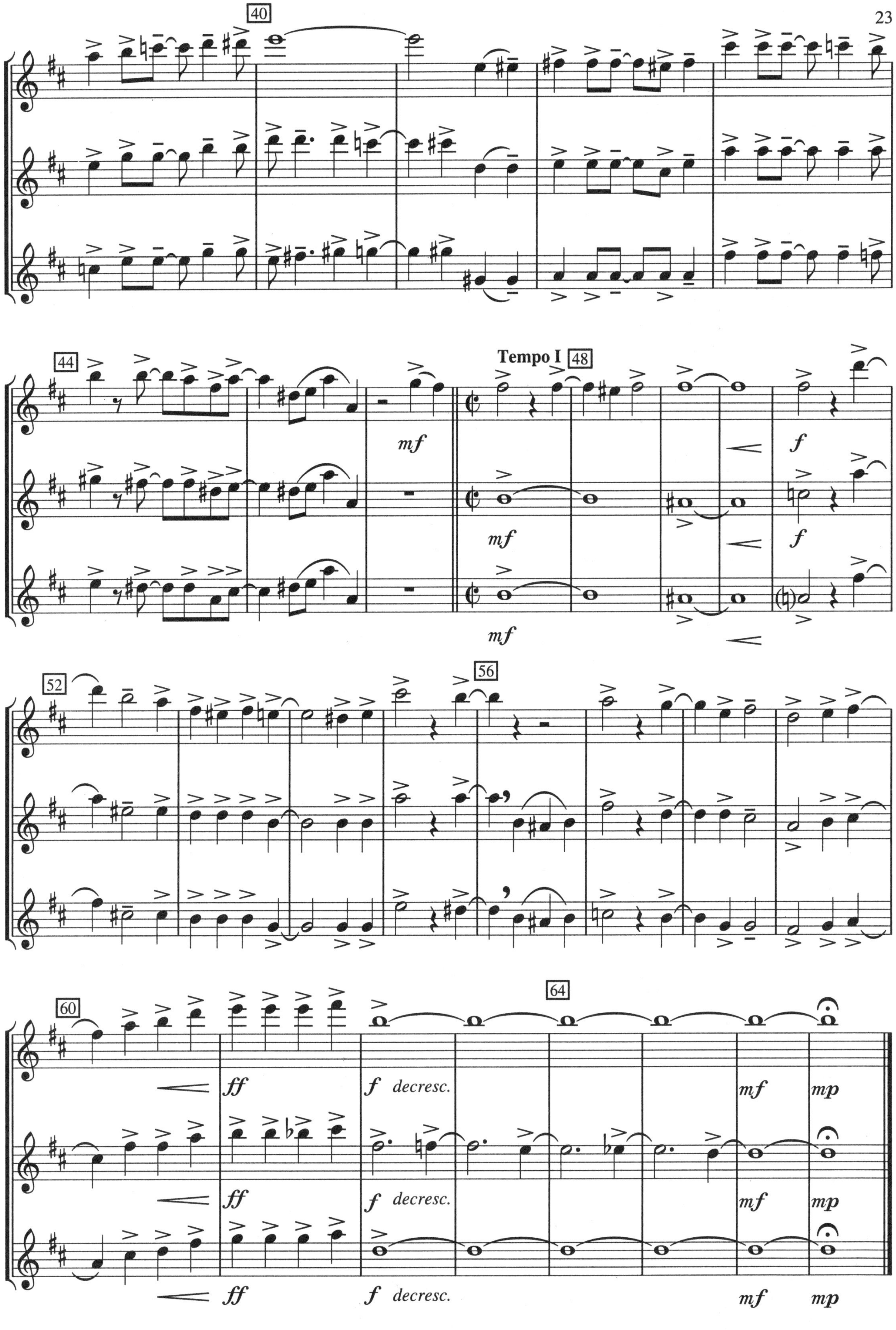
40
44
Tempo I
48
mf
f
52
56
60
64
ff
f decresc.
mf
mp

LET'S DO IT
(Let's Fall in Love)

Eb ALTO SAXOPHONE

Words and Music by
COLE PORTER
Arranged by TONY ESPOSITO

Let's Do It - 2 - 2
IF9810

LET'S MISBEHAVE

Eb ALTO SAXOPHONE

Words and Music by
COLE PORTER
Arranged by TONY ESPOSITO

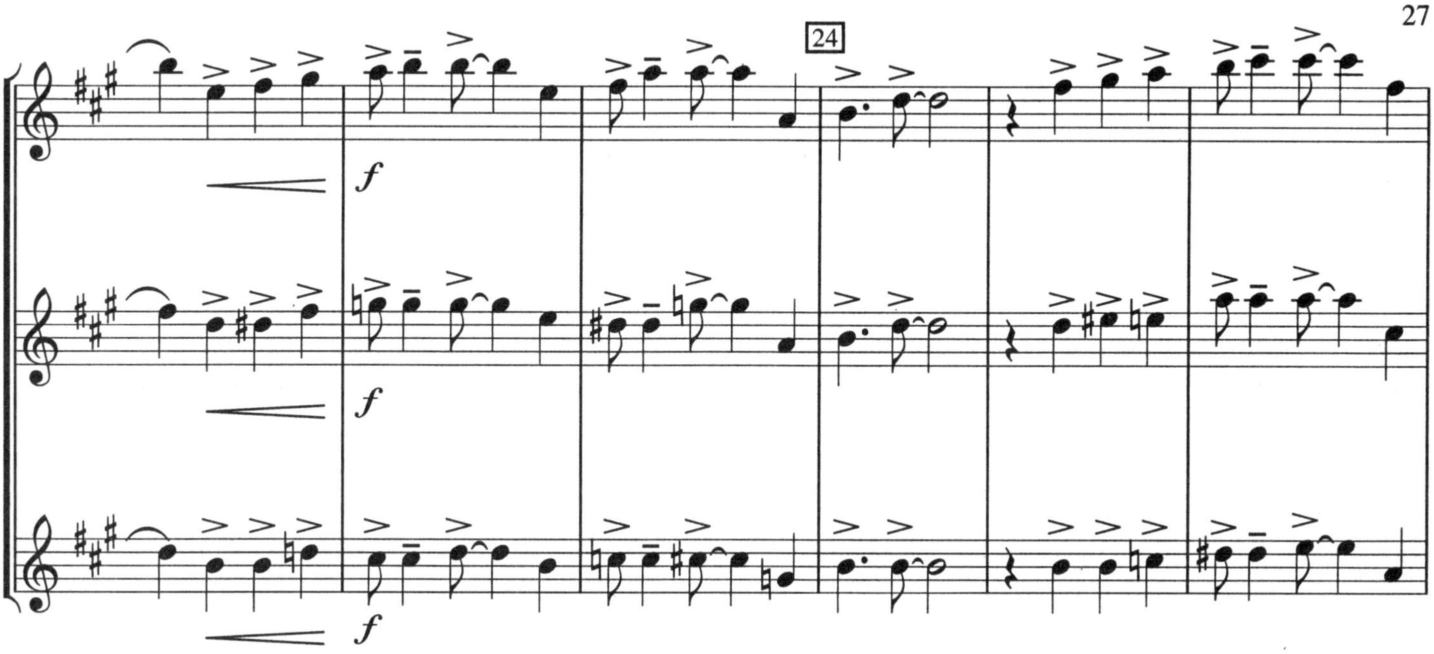
24
f
f
f

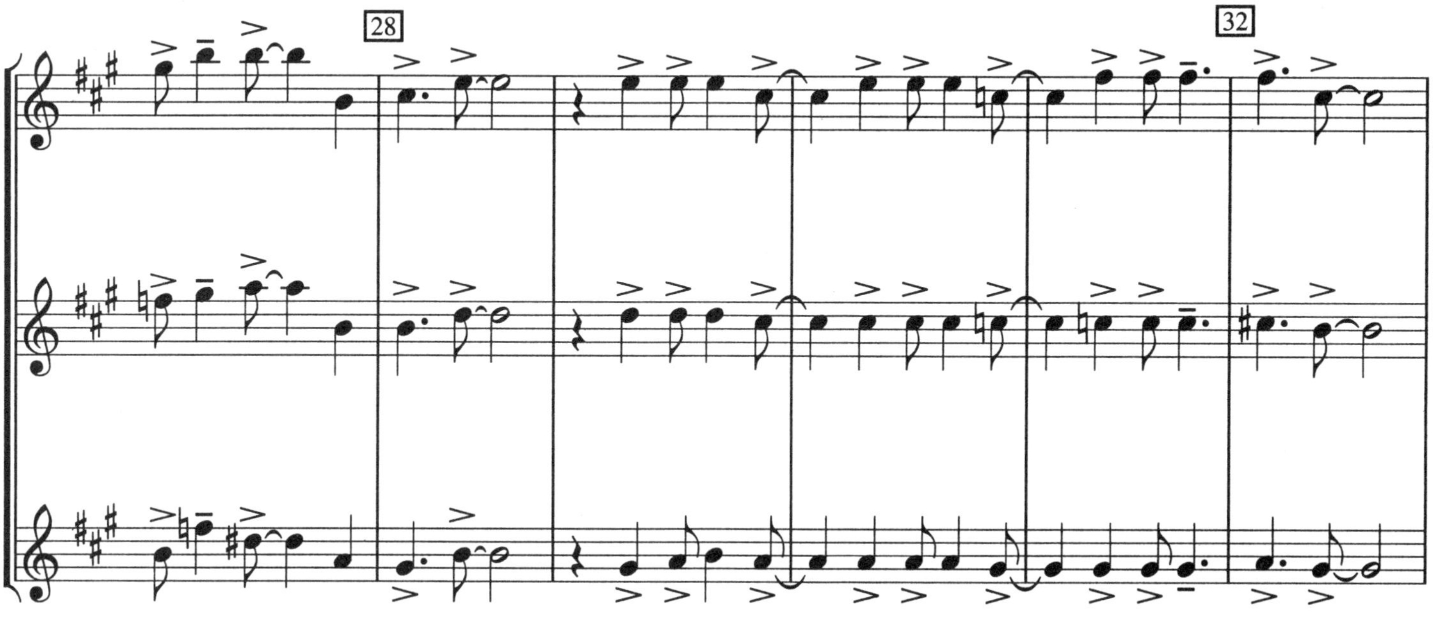
28
32

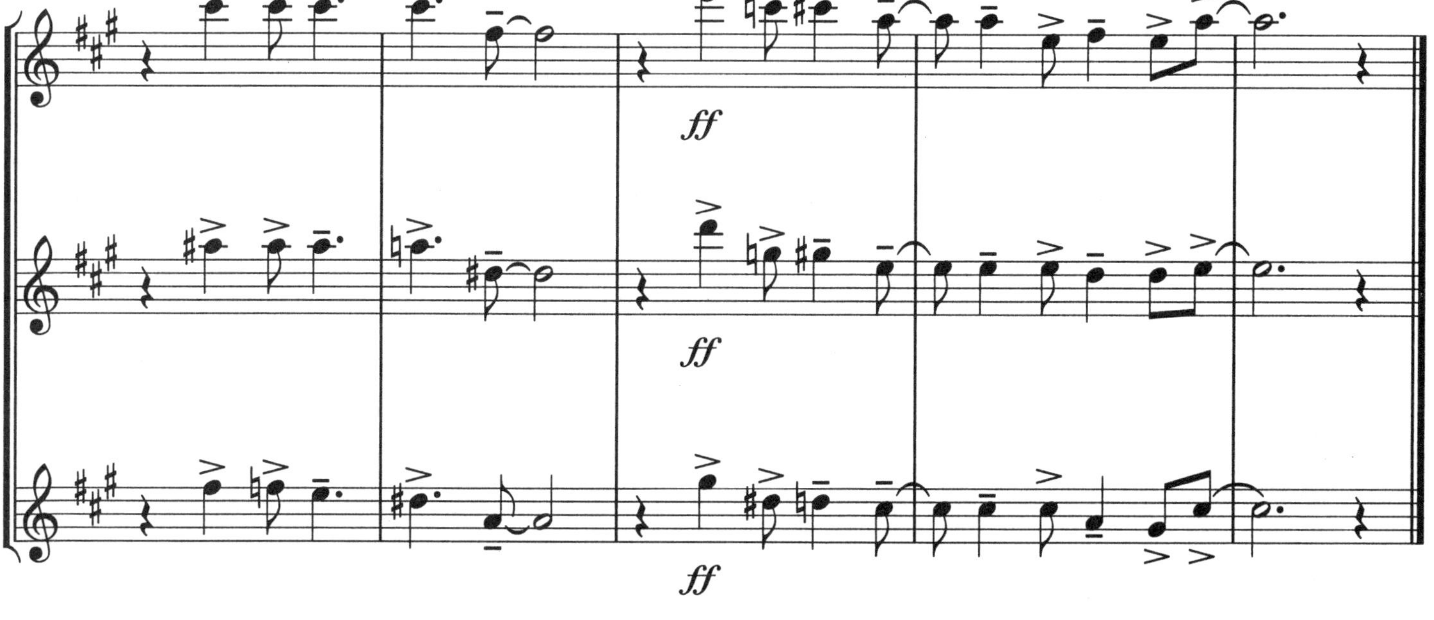
ff
ff
ff

NIGHT AND DAY

Eb ALTO SAXOPHONE
French Version by
EMELIA RENAUD
Moderately

Words and Music by
COLE PORTER
Arranged by TONY ESPOSITO

Night and Day - 2 - 2
IF9810

WHAT IS THIS THING CALLED LOVE?

Eb ALTO SAXOPHONE

Words and Music by
COLE PORTER
Arranged by TONY ESPOSITO

Swing
20
f
f
f
Solo
no solo
24
Tempo I
mf
mf
mf
28
32
ff
ff
ff
sffz
sffz
sffz

YOU DO SOMETHING TO ME

E♭ ALTO SAXOPHONE

Words and Music by
COLE PORTER
Arranged by TONY ESPOSITO

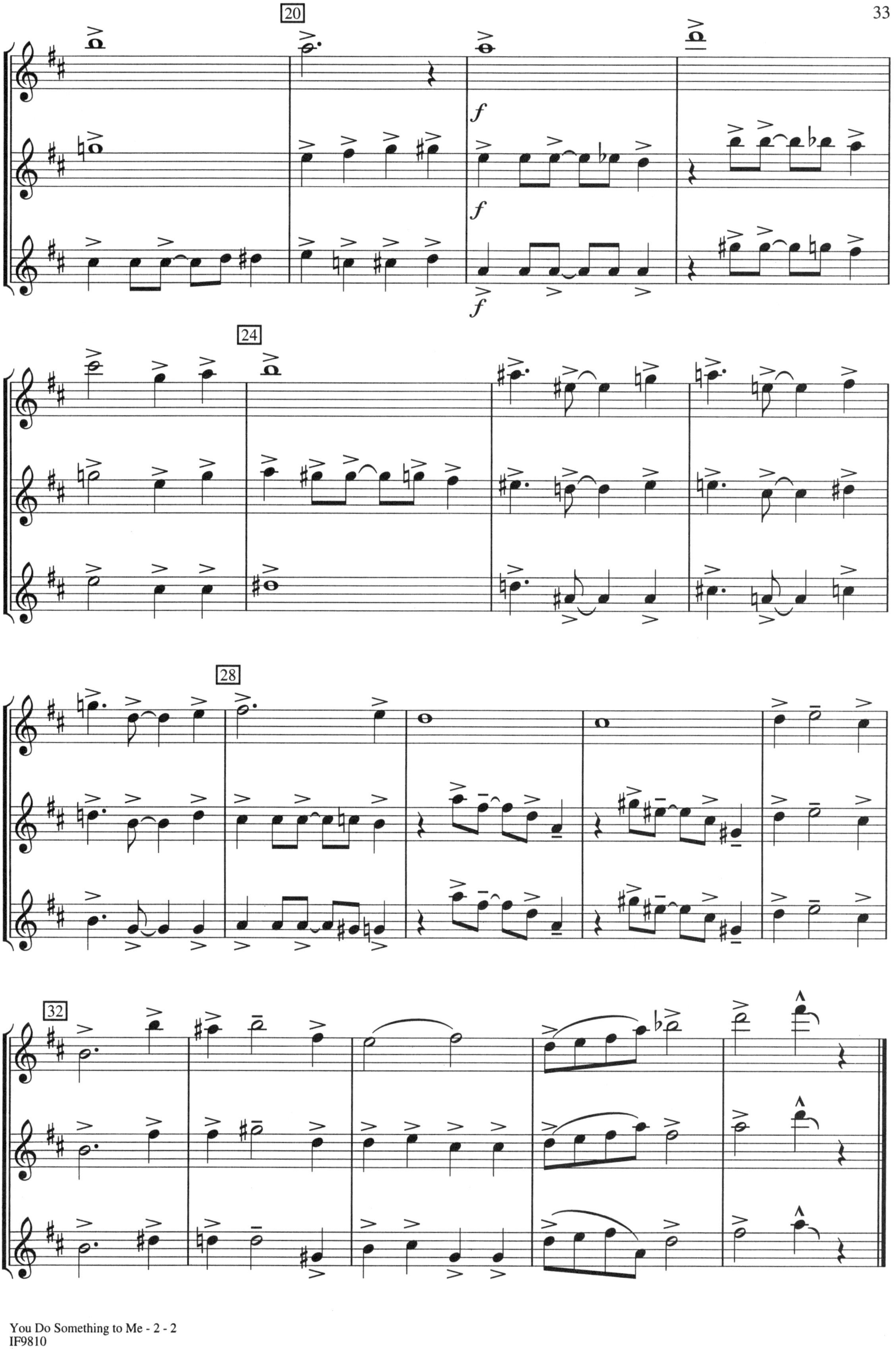
20
f
f
f
24
28
32

YOU'RE THE TOP

Eb ALTO SAXOPHONE

Words and Music by
COLE PORTER
Arranged by TONY ESPOSITO

20
mf
mp
mp
24
28
mf
mp
mf
mf
mp
mf
32
f
f
f
cresc. poco a poco
ff
sffz
cresc. poco a poco
ff
sffz
cresc. poco a poco
ff
sffz

YOU'VE GOT THAT THING

E♭ ALTO SAXOPHONE

Words and Music by
COLE PORTER
Arranged by TONY ESPOSITO

You've Got That Thing - 2 - 1
IF9810

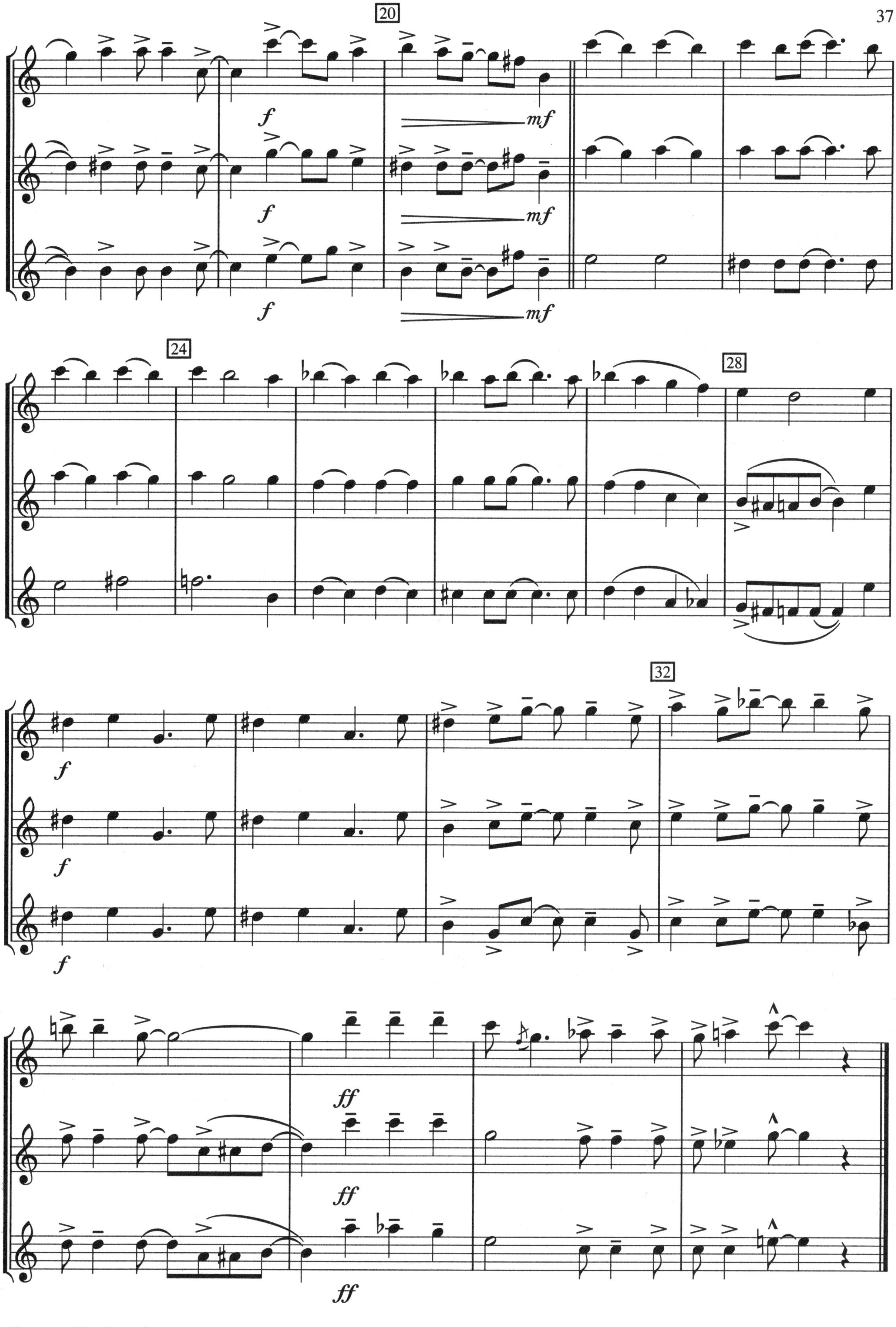
20
f
mf
f
mf
f
mf
24
28
32
f
f
f
ff
ff
ff

LOVE FOR SALE

Eb ALTO SAXOPHONE

Words and Music by
COLE PORTER
Arranged by TONY ESPOSITO

Love for Sale - 3 - 1
IF9810

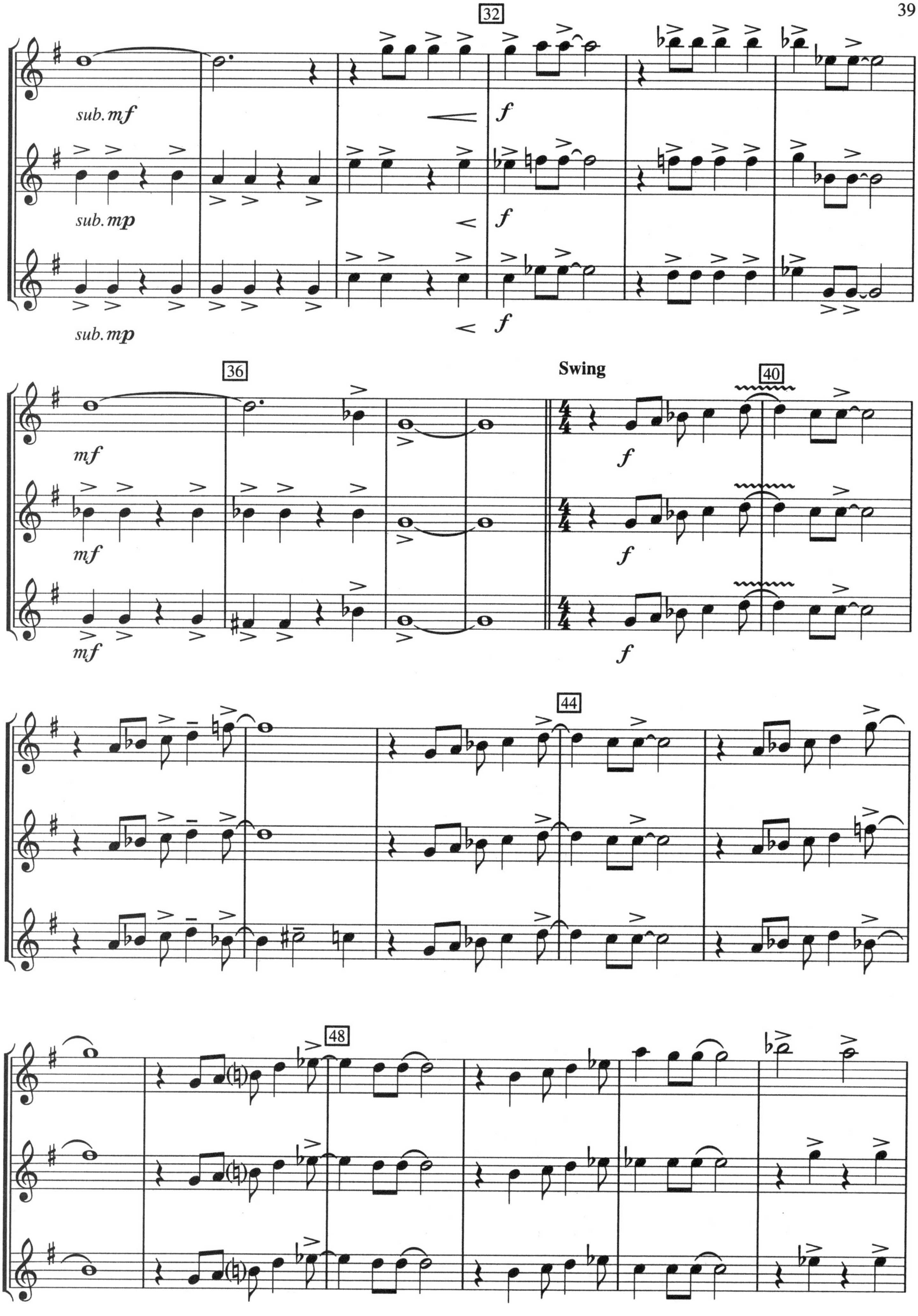
32
sub. mf
f
sub. mp
f
sub. mp
f
36
Swing
40
mf
f
mf
f
mf
f
44
48

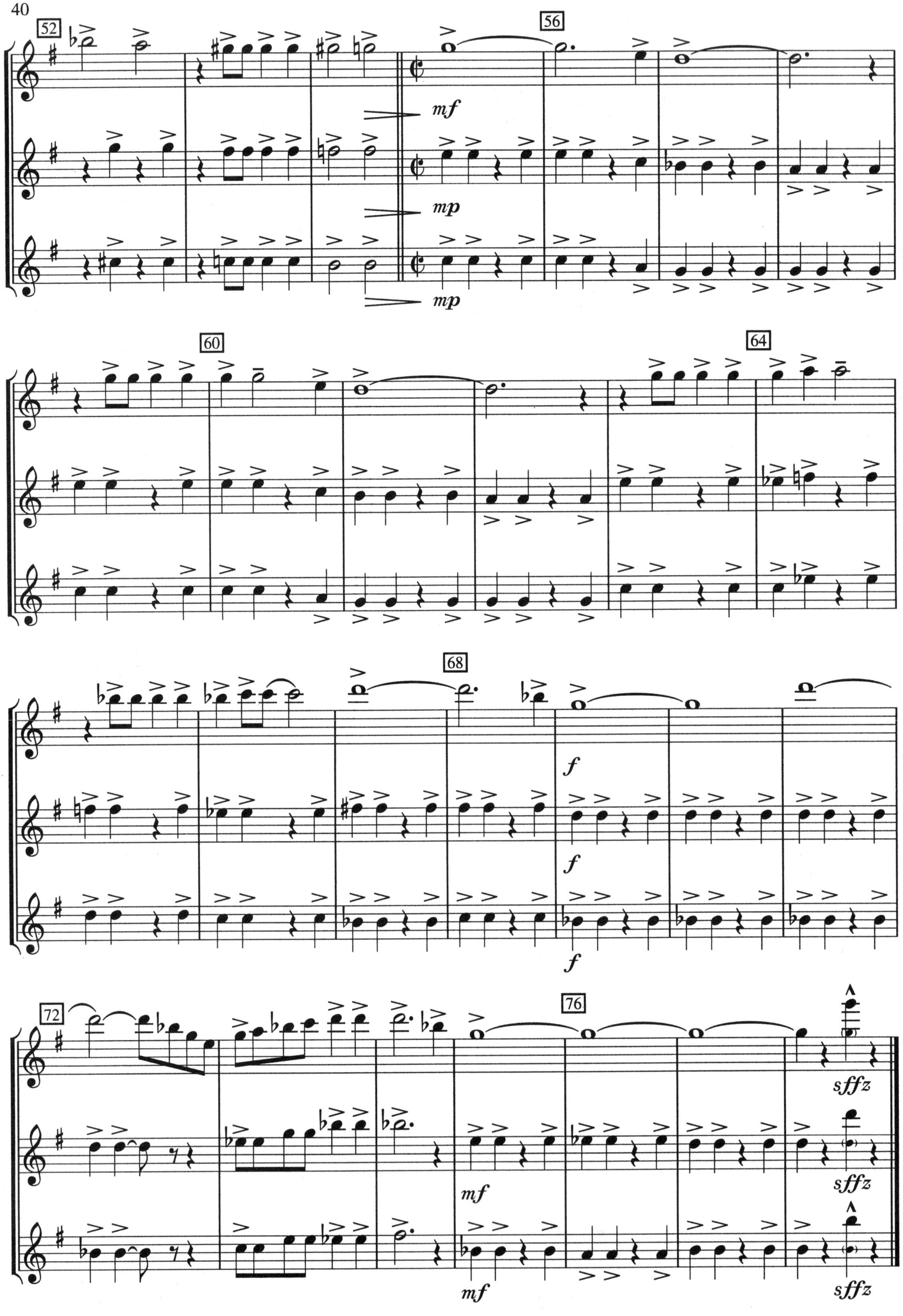
52
56
mf
mp
mp
60
64
68
f
f
f
72
76
mf
mf
sffz
sffz
sffz